# Bites, Frights, and Other Delights

**A SPOOK-TACULAR COOKBOOK**

Best.
Recipes
.co

**Food Team**
Drew Maresco
Dallyn Maresco
Melanie Stansbury

**Photography**
Drew Maresco
Dallyn Maresco

**Editorial and Proof**
Dallyn Maresco

**Layout and Design**
Drew Maresco

# Bites, Frights, and Other Delights

## A SPOOK-TACULAR COOKBOOK

FROM THE EDITORS OF THE
BEST RECIPES TEST KITCHEN

# Best Recipes .co

Copyright © 2020 by Best Recipes Media Group, LLC

All rights reserved. No part of this book may be reproduced or used, in any form or by any means, electronic or mechanical, without the permission in writing from the publisher.

Published in the United States by Best Recipes Media Group, LLC

www.bestrecipes.co

Some photographs and recipes in this book originally appeared in previous publications of Best Recipes Magazine.

ISBN 978-0-9987812-9-7

Printed in the USA

Cover and Book Design by Drew Maresco

10 9 8 7 6 5 4 3 2 1

First Edition

Illustrations by rawpixel.com / Freepik

# LOVE THESE RECIPES?
## CHECK OUT MORE FROM BEST RECIPES!

For more dinner inspiration, look for our other publications at **store.bestrecipes.co** and through various online retailers.

available at
## amazon

# Contents

| | |
|---|---|
| Introduction ................................................. 9 | Hidden Poison Cookies .......................... 31 |
| Cheeseball Brain ..................................... 11 | Cookies and Scream Franken-Puddings 33 |
| Deviled Spider Eggs ............................... 13 | Bat Truffles ............................................... 35 |
| Halloween Cheese Crackers ................. 15 | Crispy Treat .............................................. 37 |
| Franken-Guac ......................................... 17 | Brains and Pumpkins ............................. 37 |
| Mummy Brie ............................................. 19 | Monster Balls .......................................... 39 |
| Mummy Wrapped Jalapeño Poppers .... 21 | Chocolate Cake Mummy Pops .............. 41 |
| Severed Hand Meatloaf ......................... 23 | Pumpkin Seeds Sweet and Savory ....... 43 |
| Stuffed Pepper Jack-O-Lanterns ................................... 25 | Blood Shots .............................................. 45 |
| Pasta-a-la-Stein ...................................... 27 | Zombie Juice ............................................ 47 |
| Cauldron Beef and Bean Chili ............... 29 | Withches Brew ......................................... 49 |

# Introduction

Halloween is here! And who can't use a little festive inspiration every now and then? Well, this cookbook is just that!

With the spook and the fun, the bats, and the pumpkins, Halloween is always a welcomed time of year! This book will give you some creative, frightful, and spookily delicious recipes for all courses. From realistic jack-o'-lantern stuffed peppers, to deliciously bloody looking drinks, to bat truffles that may just fly off the page. This Halloween cookbook is a fun and creative outlet for kids and the kid in you. Whether you are looking for recipe inspiration for a Halloween party or just looking to have a little bit of fun with the family, these recipes will inspire some frights and delicious delights that everyone will enjoy.

So join in on the fun while exploring the wonder and excitement that Halloween can bring! Take a bite out of this ghoulish cookbook, if you dare!

 **DALLYN MARESCO**

# CHEESEBALL BRAIN

## INGREDIENTS

- 2 (8-ounce) packages cream cheese, softened
- ⅓ cup sour cream
- ½ teaspoon garlic powder
- ½ teaspoon onion powder
- ¼ teaspoon pepper
- 2 cups shredded medium cheddar cheese
- ¼ cup ketchup

## DIRECTIONS

1. In a medium bowl, add the cream cheese, sour cream, garlic powder, onion powder, and pepper. Using a hand mixer and combine until smooth.

2. Stir in the shredded cheese until fully incorporated. Cover the bowl with plastic wrap and place in the refrigerator to chill for 1 hour, or until firm.

3. Line a brain-shaped mold with plastic wrap and transfer the cheese mixture to the mold. Using a spatula, press the cheese into the mold and level off the top. Place back in the refrigerator for 1 more hour, or until firm.

4. Lift the plastic-wrapped cheeseball from the mold and unwrap. Using a clean small spoon or knife, spread the ketchup along the lines of the brain for decoration. Serve with crackers.

# DEVILED SPIDER EGGS

## INGREDIENTS

- 6 hard-boiled eggs, halved, yolks removed
- 1 small avocado, mashed
- 2 tablespoons mayo
- 2-4 drops green food dye
- Salt and pepper, to taste
- ¼ teaspoon Paprika
- 12 black olives halved

## DIRECTIONS

1. In a small bowl, stir together the egg yolks, avocado, mayo, dye, salt, pepper, and paprika until smooth. Transfer the mixture to a resealable bag, cut one corner of the bag, and pipe the mixture into the halved eggs.

2. Place an olive half onto each egg. Take the remaining olive halves and cut them into leg shapes. Place onto the eggs making spider shapes.

bestrecipes.co

# HALLOWEEN CHEESE CRACKERS

## INGREDIENTS

- 2 **cups shredded cheddar cheese**
- ¼ **cup butter, cubed**
- 1 **teaspoon salt**
- 1 **cup flour**
- 2 **tablespoons ice-cold water**

## DIRECTIONS

1. In a medium bowl, add the cheese, butter, and salt. Use a pastry cutter to combine. Add in the flour, mix until fully combined. Add the water ½ tablespoon at a time, until a dough is formed. Shape the dough into a disk and wrap with plastic wrap; refrigerate for 1 hour.

2. Preheat the oven to 375°F. Roll the dough out to ⅛-inch thick and cut into squares or use fun shaped cookie cutters. Place the cut-outs onto a baking sheet and bake for 15-20 minutes, until just browned around the edges.

# FRANKEN-GUAC

## INGREDIENTS

- 1 large avocado, mashed
- ½ lime, juiced
- ¼ cup finely minced red onion
- ⅓ cup chopped tomato (or prepared salsa)
- ½ teaspoon garlic salt
- 1 tablespoon minced fresh cilantro
- ¼ teaspoon hot sauce
- 1 (2.25-ounce) can black olives
- 1 large bag blue corn tortilla chips

## DIRECTIONS

1. In a small bowl, add the avocado, lime juice, onions, tomato, garlic salt, cilantro, and hot sauce, mashing together until fully combined.

2. On a long plate, transfer the guacamole mixture and arrange in a long rectangle shape. Take a few of the olives and make the eyes, nose, mouth, and any scars or bolts on the side. Add some chips at the top of the face to complete the Frankenstein Guacamole!

bestrecipes.co

# MUMMY BRIE

## INGREDIENTS

- 1 (8-ounce) round Brie
- 1 sheet puff pastry, thawed
- 1 egg, beaten
- 2 olives
- 1 (2.2-ounce) package of water crackers

## DIRECTIONS

1. Preheat the oven to 350°F. Using a floured rolling pin, rolling out until it's large enough to cover the brie. Place the Brie in the middle and, using a knife, cut lines around the brie, making strips. Wrap the strips over the brie and place it in a refrigerator for 30 minutes.

2. Brush the wrapped brie with the egg and cook for 30 minutes, until the puff pastry is golden brown and slightly puffed. Let rest for 5 minutes before cutting and serving with crackers.

# MUMMY WRAPPED JALAPEÑO POPPERS

## INGREDIENTS

- ½ cup cream cheese
- ½ cup shredded cheddar cheese
- 1 teaspoon paprika
- 6 large jalapeno peppers, halved lengthwise, seeds and membranes removed
- 2 tablespoons bacon bits
- 1 sheet puff pastry, cut into 12 strips, ½-inch in width

## DIRECTIONS

1. Preheat the oven to 400°F. Line a baking sheet with parchment paper.

2. In a large bowl, stir together the cream cheese, cheddar cheese, paprika, and bacon until fully combined. Fill each jalapeno half with the cheese mixture and wrap with a strip of the puff pastry. Refrigerate for 30 minutes then bake for 20 minutes, until the pastry is golden brown and puffed slightly.

bestrecipes.co

# SEVERED HAND MEATLOAF

## INGREDIENTS

- 1 cup ketchup
- 2 tablespoons mustard
- ¼ cup brown sugar
- 1 ½ pounds ground beef
- 1 egg
- ½ cup breadcrumbs
- 1 ½ teaspoons salt
- ½ teaspoon pepper
- 1 small onion, finely diced

## DIRECTIONS

1. Preheat the oven to 375°F. In a small bowl, stir together the ketchup, mustard, and brown sugar until fully combined. Set aside.

2. In a large bowl, using your hands, combine the ground beef, egg, breadcrumbs, salt, pepper, onion, and half of the prepared sauce until fully incorporated. On a parchment-lined baking sheet, shape the mixture into the shape of a hand. Optionally, reserve 5 small pieces of onion for the fingernails and place them on the fingertips. Bake for 45-50 minutes.

3. Spoon over the remaining sauce and let rest for 10 minutes before cutting and serving.

# STUFFED PEPPER JACK-O-LANTERNS

## INGREDIENTS

- 5 medium orange bell peppers, tops cut off and deseeded
- 2 cups cooked long-grain white rice
- 2 cups cooked shredded chicken
- 1 (14-ounce) can tomato sauce
- 1 (14.5-ounce) can diced fire-roasted tomatoes
- 2 teaspoons salt
- 2 teaspoons chili powder
- 1 teaspoon paprika
- 1 teaspoon garlic powder
- 1 teaspoon onion powder
- 1 cup shredded Colby cheese

## DIRECTIONS

1. Preheat the oven to 400°F. Cut the faces into the peppers. Place peppers in a baking dish and cook for 20 minutes. Remove from the oven and let rest for 5 minutes, or until cool enough to handle.

2. In a medium bowl, stir together the rice, shredded chicken, tomato sauce, diced tomatoes, salt, chili powder, paprika, garlic powder, and onion powder.

3. Fill the peppers with the rice mixture and top with cheese. Bake for 20 minutes, until the cheese is fully melted and slightly browned.

# PASTA-A-LA-STEIN

## INGREDIENTS

- 1 (16-ounce) box rotini pasta
- 1 tablespoon canola oil
- 1 garlic clove, peeled
- 1 cup fresh spinach
- 2 cups fresh basil leaves
- ¼ cup toasted pine nuts or walnuts
- ½ cup extra virgin olive oil
- ¼ cup parmesan cheese, freshly grated
- Salt and pepper, to taste
- 1 (10-ounce) mini salami, diced
- 1 red bell pepper, diced
- 1 cucumber, diced, reserving a 2-inch end
- 1 (12-ounce) container small ball mozzarella, halved
- 1 (2.25-ounce) can black olives

## DIRECTIONS

1. In a large pot over high heat, bring water to a boil and cook the pasta according to package directions. Drain and return to the pot, add the canola oil and toss to coat.

2. In a food processor, fitted with an "S" blade, add the garlic, spinach, basil, nuts, and 1 tablespoon of the olive oil. Pulse until finely chopped. Start the food processor and pour the rest of the oil in a slow, steady stream. Add the parmesan, salt, and pepper; pulse until fully combined.

3. Reserve two olives, two mozzarella halves, one piece of salami, the end of the cucumber, and a slice of the red pepper for decorating at the end. Add the pesto to the pasta, as well as the salami, pepper, cucumber, and mozzarella, tossing to fully coat. On a large plate, scoop the pasta to the plate in a rectangle shape, add the olives to the top to make the hair. Decorate and serve.

bestrecipes.co

# CAULDRON BEEF AND BEAN CHILI

### INGREDIENTS

- 1 tablespoon canola oil
- 2 pounds ground beef
- 1 green bell pepper, diced
- 1 medium onion, diced
- 2 (14-ounce) cans kidney beans, drained
- 2 (14-ounce) cans pinto beans, drained
- 1 (14-ounce) can crushed tomatoes
- 1 (6-ounce) can tomato paste
- 1 (24-ounce) can tomato juice
- 1 tablespoon chili powder
- 2 teaspoon salt
- 1 teaspoon pepper

### DIRECTIONS

1. In a large dutch oven or pot over medium-high heat, warm the oil. Add the ground beef, cooking for 7-8 minutes, until no longer pink.

2. Reduce the heat to medium-low, stir in the bell peppers, onions, beans, tomatoes, tomato paste, tomato juice, chili powder, salt, and pepper. Bring to a simmer and cover, cooking for 45 minutes. Uncover, stir, and cook for 10 minutes. Serve in cauldrons or bowls.

bestrecipes.co

# HIDDEN POISON COOKIES

### GREEN

- 2 cups flour
- 1½ teaspoon baking powder
- ½ teaspoon salt
- 1 cup sugar
- ½ cup unsalted butter, room temperature
- 2 eggs, room temperature
- Green food dye, to the desired color
- 1 teaspoon vanilla extract
- ½ teaspoon almond extract

### BLACK

- 1 cups flour
- ¾ teaspoon baking powder
- ¼ teaspoon salt
- ½ cup sugar
- ¼ cup unsalted butter, room temperature
- 1 egg, room temperature
- Black food dye, to the desired color
- ¼ teaspoon vanilla extract

### DIRECTIONS

1. In a medium bowl, combine the flour, baking powder, and salt.

2. In another medium bowl, using a hand mixer, cream together the butter and sugar, until light and fluffy. Add the eggs, one at a time, mixing well after each addition. Add the extracts and food dye, mixing again until smooth and the mix is fully colored. Add the flour mixture, combining until the dough comes together. Refrigerate the dough for 30 minutes. Repeat with the black cookie dough.

3. Preheat the oven to 350°F. Using a cookie scoop, scoop the green dough into 1-inch balls. Scoop the black dough into half size balls, using floured hands, form into disks and wrap around the green balls and place on a parchment-lined baking sheet 2-inches apart, and gently press each ball down slightly. Bake for 16 minutes. Place on a cooling rack for 15 minutes before serving.

bestrecipes.co

# COOKIES AND SCREAM FRANKEN-PUDDINGS

## INGREDIENTS

- ¾ cup sugar
- 4 tablespoons cornstarch
- 3 cups milk
- 1 teaspoon vanilla extract
- Green food coloring
- 1 package, chocolate sandwich cookies, crushed (such as Oreos®)

## DIRECTIONS

1. In a medium saucepan, stir together the sugar and cornstarch. Gradually stir in the milk and continue whisking until smooth. Turn the heat to low and bring to a simmer, stirring constantly until thickened. Remove from the heat, stir in the vanilla extract and food coloring. Cover and refrigerate until chilled.

2. Using a permanent marker, draw faces on the sides of 4 small, clear plastic cups. Add the pudding to the cups, leaving about a ½-1-inch of free space from the top. Pour the cookie crumbs over the top and serve.

bestrecipes.co

# BAT TRUFFLES

## INGREDIENTS

- 30 chocolate sandwich cookies (such as Oreos®)
- 1 (8-ounce) package of cream cheese, softened
- 6 ounces semi-sweet chocolate chips
- 2 tablespoons coconut oil
- 12 chocolate sandwich cookies, frosting removed, broken in half
- 24 candy eyes

## DIRECTIONS

1. In a food processor, fitted with an "S" blade, pulse the cookies into a powder. Add the cream cheese to the ground cookies and pulse until fully combined. Refrigerate for 1 hour.

2. Using a cookie scoop, scoop and roll into 1-inch balls. Place back in the refrigerator for 10 minutes. Add the chocolate chips and coconut oil to a medium bowl and microwave in 15-second intervals, until melted.

3. Using a fork, dip and roll the balls in the chocolate and set on a parchment-lined baking sheet. Before the chocolate hardens, place the candy eyes in the middle and insert the halved cookies into the sides, making wings. Refrigerate for 1 hour or until the chocolate is hardened

# CRISPY TREAT BRAINS AND PUMPKINS

## INGREDIENTS

- 4 tablespoons butter
- 5 cups mini marshmallows
- 6 cups crispy rice cereal
- Red food dye, to the desired color, for brains

OR

- Red and yellow food dye, to the desired color, for pumpkins

## DIRECTIONS

1. In a large pot over medium heat, melt the butter. Add the marshmallows, stirring constantly until fully melted. Stir in the food dye. Remove from heat and pour in the cereal, stirring to combine. Spray a sheet of wax paper with non-stick cooking spray, pour the mixture onto the paper and flatten with a lightly sprayed spoon; let cool for 5-10 minutes. Once cooled, you can begin forming the brains or using a cookie cutter to cut out the pumpkins. Optionally, use green food dye for the stem of the pumpkin.

# MONSTER BALLS

## INGREDIENTS

- 16 ounces candy corn
- 16 ounces peanut butter
- 3 cups chocolate chips
- Colored sprinkles
- Candy eyes

## DIRECTIONS

1. In a medium saucepan over medium heat, melt the candy corn, stirring constantly. Stir in the peanut butter until fully combined. Allow the mixture to cool slightly. Using gloves, form the mixture into 1-inch balls and transfer parchment-lined to a baking sheet.

2. In a medium bowl, add the chocolate chips and microwave in 15-second intervals, until melted. Dip each ball into the chocolate then roll in the sprinkles. Add a small amount of chocolate to the back of the candy eyes and place as desired; allow to harden before serving.

# CHOCOLATE CAKE MUMMY POPS

## INGREDIENTS

- 1    prepared chocolate cake
- 1    container chocolate frosting
- 1    (12-ounce) package white chocolate
- 24   candy eyes

## DIRECTIONS

1. Using your favorite chocolate cake recipe, bake according to the instructions and let it cool completely.

2. In a large bowl, crumble the cake and add the frosting, stir until the mixture can be molded. Using a small ice cream scoop, scoop out even balls; using your hands, roll them to be equally round balls. Chill for 10 minutes before decorating.

3. In a small bowl, microwave the chocolate in 15-second intervals, until melted. Dip one end of each of the sticks into the chocolate and skewer the cake pops, allowing the stick to stay in the pop. Once all the sticks are in the pops, pour the chocolate into a frosting bag or baggie, cut off one end, and zig-zag the chocolate around the balls, making a mummy wrapping. Add the eyes before the chocolate hardens. Let harden completely before serving.

bestrecipes.co

# PUMPKIN SEEDS SWEET AND SAVORY

## INGREDIENTS

- Seeds from a carved pumpkin, cleaned and dried
- 1 tablespoon canola oil
- 1 tablespoon season salt
- 2 teaspoons chili powder
- 1 teaspoon garlic powder
- ½ teaspoon paprika

## DIRECTIONS

1. Preheat the oven to 350°F. Place the seeds on a parchment-lined baking sheet. Drizzle oil over the seeds and sprinkle with the seasoning salt, chili powder, garlic, and paprika, tossing to evenly coat. Bake for 15 minutes. Let cool and serve.

## INGREDIENTS

- Seeds from a carved pumpkin, cleaned and dried
- 1 tablespoon canola oil
- 1 tablespoon cinnamon
- 1 tablespoon cinnamon
- ⅓ cup brown sugar

## DIRECTIONS

1. Preheat the oven to 350°F. Place the seeds on a parchment-lined baking sheet. Drizzle oil over the seeds and sprinkle with the cinnamon and brown sugar, tossing to evenly coat. Bake for 15 minutes. Let cool and serve.

# BLOOD SHOTS

## INGREDIENTS

- 1 (2-liter) bottle lemon-lime soda
- 16 ounces berry vodka
- 8 ounces grenadine

## DIRECTIONS

1. In 8 serving cups, combine 1 cup of soda with 2 ounces of vodka. Serve with 1 ounce of grenadine on the side to be added for the bloody effect.

**Note:** For a non-alcoholic beverage, remove the vodka to make it virgin.

bestrecipes.co

# ZOMBIE JUICE

## INGREDIENTS

- 1 (2-liter) bottle lemon-lime soda
- ⅓ cup grenadine
- 1½ quarts lime sherbert
- 1 (12-ounce) can frozen limeade concentrate, thawed

## DIRECTIONS

1. Pour the soda into the brain mold, leaving about 1-inch of space from the top. Add the grenadine to the mold and stir to combine. Freeze for 6 hours, or overnight.

2. In a large punch bowl, add the remaining lemon-lime soda and the limeade concentrate, stirring until fully mixed. Add half of the sherbet in scoops and stir, letting sit for 30 minutes. Add the frozen brain, remaining sherbet, and serve.

# WITHCHES BREW

**INGREDIENTS**

    Handful of ice
4  shots berry vodka
6  ounces blue curaçao
4  ounces grenadine
    A splash of lime juice
    Purple sugar

**DIRECTIONS**

1. In a mixing jar, add the ice, vodka, blue curacao, grenadine, and lime juice, cover, and shake. Line the edge of the martini glasses with lime juice and coat the edge with purple sugar. Evenly pour into two martini glasses. Serve.

bestrecipes.co

# INDEX

Cheeseball Brain    11

Deviled Spider Eggs    13

Halloween Cheese Crackers    15

Franken-Guac    17

Mummy Brie    19

Mummy Wrapped Jalapeño Poppers    21

Severed Hand Meatloaf    23

Stuffed Pepper Jack-O-Lanterns    25

Pasta-a-la-Stein    27

Cauldron Beef and Bean Chili    29

Hidden Poison Cookies    31

Cookies and Scream Franken-Puddings    33

Bat Truffles
35

Crispy Treat Brains and Pumpkins
37

Monster Balls
39

Chocolate Cake Mummy Pops
41

Pumpkin Seeds Sweet and Savory
43

Blood Shots
45

Zombie Juice
47

Withches Brew
49

# ABOUT THE AUTHORS

**DREW MARESCO**

Author and self-taught cook with a mind for creating unique, simple, and delicious recipes. Inspired at a young age while sitting on grandma's countertop, he assisted with everything she baked. After starting what began as a small food blog, to what is now the website and various print publications of BestRecipes.co, he strives to make dinner simple and easy for everyone.

**DALLYN MARESCO**

Starting as a writer, then editor and food stylist, she loves the art behind everything that she does. Learning how to cook came at a young age baking with grandma, which became one of her favorite things. Her writing background is what brought her to the food team at Best Recipes, quickly becoming an integral part of the operations, and her work is seen in every recipe we publish.

# STILL HUNGRY?

Well, there's plenty more where that came from!
For more recipes, books, videos, and more, visit

## BESTRECIPES.CO

## ABOUT BEST RECIPES

Best Recipes Media Group develops both print and digital resources to help busy people get back into the kitchen and make their own meals with recipes that are quick and easy for everyone, regardless of cooking skill.

www.ingramcontent.com/pod-product-compliance
Lightning Source LLC
Chambersburg PA
CBHW061146010526
44118CB00026B/2883